STATE OF VERMONT
DEPARTMENT OF LIBRARIES
NORTHWEST REGIONAL LIBRARY
RFD #2
FAIRFAX, VERMONT 0545

WITHDRAWN

VERMONT DEPARTMENT OF LIBRARIES
MIDSTATE REGIONAL LIBRARY
RR #4, BOX 1870
MONTPELIER, VERMONT 05602

C0-DAT-963

ROCK CLIMBING
is for me

ROCK CLIMBING
is for me

Tom Hyden
and Tim Anderson

photographs by
Bob and Diane Wolfe

 Lerner Publications Company   Minneapolis

Special thanks to the Science Museum of Minnesota, Jane Neumann, Eastern Mountain Sports, Inc., Laura Storms, Rochelle, Jason, Neil, Erik, Kevin, Greg, Jed, George, Nathan, Brad, Dale, and Chris

LIBRARY OF CONGRESS CATALOGING IN PUBLICATION DATA

Hyden, Tom.
   Rock climbing is for me.

   (A Sports for me book)
   Summary: A young girl describes her experiences learning to rock climb. Includes safety tips, information on climbing techniques and equipment, and a glossary of terms.
   1. Rock climbing—Juvenile literature. 2. Rock climbing—Safety measures—Juvenile literature.
   [1. Rock climbing] I. Anderson, Tim, 1948—
   II. Wolfe, Robert L., ill. III. Wolfe, Diane, ill.
   IV. Title. V. Series: Sports for me books.
   GV200.2.H93   1984   796.5'223'0289   84-2906
   ISBN 0-8225-1147-9 (lib. bdg.)

Copyright © 1984 by Lerner Publications Company

All rights reserved. International copyright secured. No part of this book may be reproduced in any form whatsoever without permission from the publisher except for the inclusion of brief quotations in an acknowledged review.

Manufactured in the United States of America

International Standard Book Number: 0-8225-1147-9
Library of Congress Catalog Card Number: 84-2906

1 2 3 4 5 6 7 8 9 10 93 92 91 90 89 88 87 86 85 84

Hi! My name is Rochelle, or Shelly for short. This is my brother Jason. Our favorite sport is rock climbing. Our older brother Tom is a rock climber, and he promised to teach us how to climb as soon as we were old enough.

Rock climbing is an exciting sport. You try to work your way up the side of a cliff by gripping onto rocks with your hands and feet. To be a good rock climber, you have to concentrate very hard on what you're doing. It takes skill and practice to make your way up the side of a steep cliff.

Jason and I joined a rock climbing class for beginners. The class was being taught by Tom and his friend Tim. Our first class was held at a sporting goods store. At the store there was a 25-foot-high fireplace chimney specially built for climbing. The chimney was made of stone and was *very* steep! It was a good place to practice for a real outdoor climb.

At our first class, Tom explained some
rock climbing basics. First, he told us that
the most important thing in rock climbing
is safety. Rock climbing should only be
attempted if you've had some lessons. And
there *must* be an experienced, older rock
climber present at all times.

Next, Tom told us about the ropes used for rock climbing. When climbing, he explained, ropes are used for the climber's protection.

Most climbers use **kernmantle ropes**. They are very strong and will stretch to cushion a fall. A kernmantle rope has an inner core of nylon fibers with a woven covering. Climbers are always careful to step *over* their ropes, never on them. If you step on a rope, small pieces of rock and dirt can be pushed into it. This will cut the fibers and weaken the rope.

Before each climb, the ropes are set up in a special way. First, very strong straps called **webbing** are attached to an immovable object, like a tree or a rock, at the top of the cliff. The tree or rock is called an **anchor**.

The webbing is attached to an aluminum clip called a **carabiner** (CARE-uh-BEE-nur), or biner for short. Carabiners are something like safety pins because they have a gate that opens and then snaps shut.

The rope is then passed through the carabiner, and the two ends of the rope dangle down the side of the cliff. One end of the rope is tied to the climber. The other end is tied to the adult rock climber who is there to handle the ropes and protect the climber from falling. This person is called the **belayer**.

The belayer's job is to keep the rope **taut**, or pulled tight, to help prevent the climber from falling and to help stop a fall if the climber should slip. The belayer stands at the bottom of the cliff. As the climber moves upward, the rope slips through the carabiner, and the belayer pulls in the slack rope.

Tom and Tim showed us the special knot used to connect the ropes to the climber. This knot is called a **bowline (BO-lin)-on-a-coil**. To tie the bowline-on-a-coil, Tom wrapped the rope around his waist three times and then made a loop in his right hand. He tucked the loop under the three coils and threaded the end in and out of the loop. Finally, he tied two safety overhand knots around the coil.

The bowline-on-a-coil is a good knot for climbing. It won't come undone but is easy to untie when you're through with your climb. We all picked up a rope to practice.

The belayer uses a bowline knot, too. This knot is similar to the bowline-on-a-coil, but only wraps once around the waist.

The belayer also uses the **figure eight** knot. The figure eight knot looks something like the number 8 when it's tied properly. It is used to attach the rope and webbing to an anchor. The anchor will keep the belayer positioned correctly.

We practiced the bowline-on-a-coil, bowline, and figure eight several times. We practiced the bowline-on-a-coil especially hard, but we really wouldn't be doing much belaying until we were older.

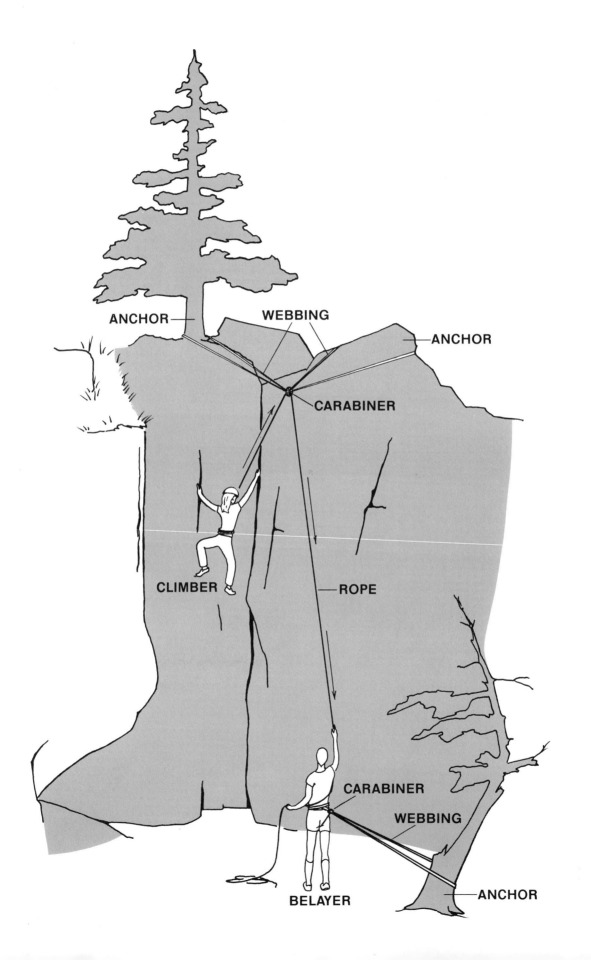

ANCHOR

WEBBING

ANCHOR

CARABINER

CLIMBER

ROPE

CARABINER

WEBBING

BELAYER

ANCHOR

Next we learned the **commands** a climber and belayer use to talk with each other while climbing. Since the climber and belayer are often far apart, the commands must be short and easy to understand. Every command called out by the climber has to be answered by the belayer before the climber can make a move or go on to the next command. These are the commands that are exchanged during every climb:

PERSON	COMMAND	MEANING
Climber	**ON BELAY**	Are you ready?
Belayer	**BELAY ON**	Yes.
Climber	**CLIMBING**	I'm starting.
Belayer	**CLIMB ON**	Go ahead.
Climber	**OFF BELAY**	I've reached the top.
Belayer	**BELAY OFF**	O.K.
Climber	**THANK YOU**	You prevented me from falling.

We also learned three extra commands to use during certain climbing situations:

PERSON	COMMAND	MEANING
Climber	**SLACK**	Let out some rope.
Climber	**TENSION**	Pull up the slack rope.
Climber	**FALLING**	I'm falling.

When Tom and Tim thought we knew the commands, they said it was time to try our first climb. We were so excited! Jason was going to be first, so we all watched carefully as he got ready. Tom checked Jason's knots and reminded him to find a helmet. Rock climbers *always* wear helmets to protect their heads from injury in case they slip or get hit by a falling rock.

The rope at the sporting goods store ran through carabiners that were attached to a wooden beam in the ceiling. When one end of the rope was correctly tied around Jason's waist and the other end around Tom's, Jason was ready. He said "On belay," and Tom answered "Belay on." Then Jason called out "Climbing!" and when Tom answered "Climb on," Jason made his first moves.

Tom told Jason to take plenty of time between moves. Rock climbing is not a race. The important thing is to find secure **holds** for your hands and feet.

A hold is any rock big enough to be gripped by hand or foot. A large hold is called a **bucket**. A **finger hold** may only be big enough for two or three fingers. Once you've found a good hand- or foothold, you're ready for your next move.

Jason made it all the way up to the top! At the top of the climb there was a cement ledge. Jason said it was nice to have the ledge to rest on. After resting, Tom lowered Jason down.

Soon it was my turn. Tom checked my knots and helped me with the helmet. We exchanged commands, and I was ready to go. First I looked for a place for my foot, and then I reached up with my hands. When I found a secure handhold, I moved my foot again. Tom reminded me that we're doing **three-point climbing**. That means finding a new hold for only one hand or foot at a time. It's like climbing a ladder.

I was about 10 feet above the floor, and all I could see was a long vertical crack. There were no other handholds or footholds to use.

For a crack like this, climbers often **jam**. Jamming is placing a hand or foot into a crack and then twisting or turning it so that it won't slip out. I put my foot into the crack and twisted it. It really worked! My foot stayed securely in the crack, and I was able to boost myself up higher. Soon I made it to the ledge. I rested a minute and then came back down.

When each of us had had a few turns climbing the chimney, Tim and Tom reminded us that our next class would be at a state park that had great cliffs for climbing. We'd be climbing a 30-foot cliff!

When the day finally came, we all piled into a van and drove to the climbing area. When we got there, Tim walked up a path to the top of the 30-foot cliff to set up the ropes. Tom took us down to the bottom of the cliff. The area at the bottom was called "The Pit."

As we explored the pit, Tom explained that the cliffs we would be climbing on are made of a hard, black rock called **basalt**. This basalt flowed out of volcanoes over one billion years ago. The river that flows through the park drained a huge lake formed from a melting glacier, and the river cut through the basalt to form these cliffs.

It is important to climb on hard rock like basalt and not on more crumbly rock like sandstone. On crumbly rocks, you can easily slip and get hurt.

While Tom and Tim got everything ready for our climb, we continued exploring the area. Rock climbing is a great way to enjoy nature. The rocks are beautiful with lots of interesting plants growing in and around them. Tom told us we must always be careful not to step on any of the plants we see. We also shouldn't disturb any insects or animals we encounter.

We saw a small blue wildflower called a harebell growing out of a crack. We also saw many **lichens** (LIE-kins). Lichens grow on rock where nothing else can live. They can be green, white, or orange and may be thousands of years old. These old and rare plants need our protection, so we have to watch our step!

Tim was almost finished setting up the ropes. He had set up two of them so that two of us could climb at the same time. For extra safety, he used two anchors and three carabiners for each rope. When he came back down, he showed us how to wrap the webbing around a big boulder. The boulder would be the belayer's anchor.

After setting up the ropes, Tom and Tim put on **seat harnesses**. Seat harnesses are often used by both climbers and belayers because they're more comfortable than the around-the-waist knots. They then attached **belay plates** to the ropes. Belay plates help to increase friction on the rope. This makes climbing safer.

29

Nathan and Chris were chosen to climb first. We all sat down to watch them. We tried to stay quiet so that they could concentrate better and hear the commands.

When my turn came, I was a little nervous. This would be my first *real* climb. But everyone wished me luck, and I was ready.

This climb had a long vertical crack. So I started my climb by jamming my hand and foot into the crack and twisting them. Next I reached out to the left to find a handhold. This worked so well that I jammed all the way to the top. I made it!

Jason went next. I helped him buckle the helmet and wished him luck. He found good handholds and made it to the top just as easily as I did.

When everyone in the class had climbed twice, we picked up all the equipment and got ready to go home. But before we left, we walked a short way to look at the cliff we would be climbing at our next class. Tom said it was about 60 feet high, but it looked like a hundred! I could hardly wait.

On the day of our next class, we arrived at the climbing area in time for lunch. As we were eating, Tim and his friend Mike walked up a trail to the top of the cliff to set up the anchors and drop down the ropes.

One of the pieces of webbing was anchored with a **hexentric nut**. This is a six-sided aluminum nut that slips into a crack but won't slip out.

This climb was steeper and had smaller holds than the 30-foot cliff. Tim climbed up first so we could get an idea of how to do it.

When Jason's turn came, Tom checked to make sure he was tied in correctly. Jason started with good toe- and handholds and **smeared** with his left foot. You smear when the rock is totally smooth and there are no bumps, ledges, or cracks to rest your feet on. To smear, place your foot on the surface of the smooth rock and put your weight on that foot to create friction. The friction helps you get a grip on the flat rock.

Jason got stuck for a few minutes, and he called down the command "Slack." Tom let out some rope so Jason could swing his foot up to a new hold. The next time I looked up, he was standing on a ledge halfway up the cliff. Then he climbed the rest of the way to the top.

Even when you reach the top of your climb, you must *never* forget about safety. You must move *well away* from the edge before removing your ropes and helmet. At our lessons, Tim's friend Mike stood at the top of the cliff to help us with the ropes and to show us the trail to take back down to the bottom.

When it was my turn, Tom gave me some directions about where to put my feet and hands. I reached high with my left leg and jammed both hands into a crack. Then I needed a place for my right foot. I found one!

When I stood up, I could see more holds above me, and the rest was easier. I could hear the rope sliding through the carabiners, so I knew I was close to the top. When I climbed over the top and had moved away from the edge, I yelled "Off belay." Everybody cheered for me. It was a great feeling.

When it was time to leave, we picked up all the equipment and litter so that we would leave the area just as we had found it. I was tired from climbing, but I was excited, too. Tom had promised to take Jason and me climbing the next weekend.

I couldn't wait to try that 60-foot cliff again, and it would be fun to spend the day with Tom and Jason.

We wanted to get an early start on Saturday, so we laid out all of our equipment on Friday night. We checked it carefully to make sure everything was in good shape and that we hadn't forgotten anything.

When we got to the climbing area, Jason and I untangled all of the webbing. Then Tom went to the top of the cliff to anchor the ropes. It took him a long time to finish, but we knew he wanted everything to be safe.

Jason got ready to climb while Tom clipped a carabiner to the anchor webbing and to his harness. We both wanted to try the same climb that we had done last week, but Jason decided to climb a new **route**. A route is the trail you follow up a cliff. A good route has many holds.

Jason's climb went very well. As I got ready to climb, Tom suggested that I try a new route, too. The first few holds were easy. Good climbers always look ahead to avoid dead ends. I tried to lean away from the rock as I climbed. When I did, I could see where I was going. Also, my weight was forced into the rock instead of straight down. This gave me better balance.

After climbing for a while, I felt my knees begin to shake. That's called "**sewing machine leg**," and it's caused by fatigue. I found a ledge to rest on. As I rested on the ledge, I looked out across the treetops. Tom and Jason looked tiny down on the ground! It was so quiet and peaceful. The only sound was the chattering of swallows chasing insects.

After my rest, I felt ready to make it to the top. I tried to lift my knee to the next ledge, but Tom yelled for me to use my foot instead. Knees are weak joints and can easily get stuck in jams. If I could swing my foot up there, I could then straighten my leg and get much higher. It worked! I was at the top. This route was harder than last week's, and I really felt good that I had made it.

We spent most of the afternoon climbing and exploring. We had a great time, but soon it was time to go home. We packed all the equipment and got ready to leave. As we were walking up the trail towards the car, Tom said he was very proud of Jason and me. He said that climbing is a sport that we can enjoy all our lives. I'm sure I will, because rock climbing is for me!

ROCK CLIMBING Words

ANCHOR: A solid, immovable object like a tree or rock to which webbing is attached

BASALT: A hard volcanic rock that is very good for climbing

BELAYER: The person who handles the ropes and protects the climber from falling

BOWLINE: A knot used by the belayer

BOWLINE-ON-A-COIL: A knot used by the climber

CARABINER: An aluminum clip used to fasten ropes to webbing and anchor points

CHOCK: A general term for a variety of metal blocks that are slipped into cracks and attached to rope and used as anchors

COMMANDS: The series of instructions called out between the climber and belayer

EDGING: Using the sides of one's shoes to stand on very narrow ledges

FIGURE EIGHT: A knot that when tied properly resembles the number 8

HEXENTRIC NUT: A six-sided aluminum nut used for anchoring webbing; a type of chock

IGNEOUS ROCK: Rock that was once molten lava, very good for climbing. Basalt and granite are two kinds of igneous rock.

HOLD: Any rock big enough to be gripped by hand or foot

JAM: To place a hand or foot into a crack and twist and turn it so it will not slip out

KERNMANTLE ROPE: A very strong, flexible rope made of an inner core of nylon fibers covered with a woven sheath

LICHEN: A very old, slow-growing, fungus-like plant that grows on rocks

SMEAR: To place the feet on the surface of a smooth rock in order to create friction

TECHNICAL ROCK BOOTS: Boots worn by rock climbers

WEBBING: Nylon straps used to anchor ropes and belayers

ABOUT THE AUTHORS

TOM HYDEN is active in several outdoor sports including rock climbing, skiing, and running. He is a naturalist/science teacher and a former elementary school teacher. Currently, Mr. Hyden is employed in the education department of the Science Museum of Minnesota in St. Paul.

TIM ANDERSON is an interpretive naturalist at the Woodlake Nature Center in Richfield, Minnesota. Along with his interest in natural history, he is an avid birdwatcher, beekeeper, and monarch butterfly bander. Mr. Anderson has been a rock climber for over seven years.

ABOUT THE PHOTOGRAPHERS

BOB AND DIANE WOLFE have a freelance photography business in Minneapolis, Minnesota. Bob studied photography at the Minneapolis College of Art and Design and was senior medical photographer at the University of Minnesota for several years. Diane worked as a nurse for many years in the Twin Cities. In addition to her interest in photography, she is an accomplished potter. The Wolfes enjoy karate, biking, camping, and canoeing.

AAA-61166

WITHDRAWN

VERMONT DEPT. OF LIBRARIES

0 00 01 0075790 5